Sweet Potato Plant

flower

leaf

stem

tuber
(sweet potato)

soil

roots

Look about you. Take hold of the things that are here. Let them talk to you. You learn to talk to them.
—George Washington Carver (c. 1864–1943)

I would like to thank Ranger Curtis Gregory
at the George Washington Carver National Monument
in Diamond, Missouri, for helping me repeatedly and cordially
as I researched and wrote this book.

I would like to dedicate this book to Executive Editor Grace Maccarone and
Art Director Claire Counihan at Holiday House for helping to bring this book
to life at long last. I first started writing it in 1995. It took me fifteen years,
working off and on, to write the final version. That's the longest any book has
ever taken me. It was worth the wait. I also want to thank
Ken Wilson-Max for his gorgeous artwork.
—J. M.

To my dad, Ken, Sr.
—K. W-M.

Text copyright © 2011 by Jean Marzollo
Illustrations copyright © 2011 by Ken Wilson-Max
All Rights Reserved
HOLIDAY HOUSE is registered in the U.S. Patent and Trademark Office.
Printed and Bound in December, 2010 at Tien Wah Press,
Johor Bahru, Johor, Malaysia.
The text typeface is Breughel.
The artwork was created with acrylic paints on paper.
www.holidayhouse.com
First Edition
1 3 5 7 9 10 8 6 4 2

Library of Congress Cataloging-in-Publication Data
Marzollo, Jean.
The little plant doctor : a story about George Washington Carver / by Jean Marzollo ; illustrated by Ken Wilson-Max.
p. cm.
ISBN 978-0-8234-2325-5 (hardcover)
1. Carver, George Washington, 1864?-1943—Juvenile literature. 2. African American agriculturists—
Biography—Juvenile literature. 3. Agriculturists—United States—Biography—Juvenile literature.
I. Wilson-Max, Ken. II. Title.
S417.C3M295 2011
630.92—dc22
[B]
2010024064

The Little Plant Doctor

A Story About George Washington Carver

by **Jean Marzollo**

illustrated by **Ken Wilson-Max**

Holiday House / New York

I'm a very old tree. I live in Diamond, Missouri. Old trees like me have stories to tell. My favorite story is about a little boy named George Carver. He came to visit me long, long ago when this place was just a farm. I was little then.

George came right up to me and said, "Little Tree, we're the same size." Then he smiled and said, "I have an idea."

George dug holes around me. He set wildflowers into the holes and talked to the plants. If a flower drooped, George asked, "What's the matter? Too much sun? Too little sun?" He moved some plants from sun to shade and others from shade to sun. He studied how much water they needed. "Do you need more water?" he asked. "Or less water?"

George studied the leaves, the
stems, the roots, and the root ball
of each plant. A root ball is the
ball of soil that clings to a plant
when it is lifted from the
ground. George handled his
plants carefully because he
didn't want any part to break.

"I wish I could go to school,"
he said. "What am I going to do,
Little Tree, if I can't go to school?
There's so much I want
to learn."

George talked with Uncle Moses. Moses Carver and his wife, Sue, owned the farm where George and his brother lived, and they took care of the boys. "Little George," he said. "You were so sick when you were a baby. You will always be too small and weak for farm life. You love plants, but you can't work in the fields with your brother and me. What will you do when you grow up?"

George said, "I really want to go to school."

"I know you do," said Uncle Moses. "But it's the eighteen seventies. The only school here is for white children. You can't go to school with them."

So George stayed home, helping with housework and studying plants. He learned how to help sick plants get better. He cured sick plants for people, like this neighbor whose flowering plant wouldn't bloom anymore. One day George told me, "Little Tree, guess what? People have started calling me the Little

George told me that Aunt Sue taught him to
read and write. She had a spelling book that George read
over and over. He loved to read.

Years passed. One day when George Carver was about twelve, he came to tell me some good news. "I'm going to school!" he told me. He said that he was going to a school eight miles away in Neosho. George gave me a hug and said, "I will miss you, Little Tree."

I was sad not to see George anymore. His garden died because nobody took care of it. How could they? No one knew where it was except me.

HO
ES

Then, one day when George Carver was a young man, he came back for a visit.

"Little Tree," he said, "you're so big now. Guess what? I'm going to college. I'm going to study painting, singing, and plant science."

George told me he had given himself a middle name. His name now was George Washington Carver.

I always wonder why George picked that middle name. I've heard some people say that he might have called himself George Washington Carver after the first president of the United States. They think that maybe he had a hunch that someday he too would be famous.

I'm just a tree so I don't know what a president is. But I do know that George Washington Carver did become famous. How do I know that? Because so many people now come to see where he grew up. The Carver farm is a big park now! It's called the George Washington Carver National Monument.

Today park rangers take people on tours through the park. They tell schoolchildren that George Washington Carver became one of the most famous scientists ever! He worked and taught at Tuskegee Institute in Alabama. He worked in a laboratory where he found new uses for peanuts and sweet potatoes. George Washington Carver was also kind. He gave his ideas away for free because he wanted to help people.

I'm glad to see that black and white children go to school together today. The children and I listen to the park ranger say, "This tree may have been little when Dr. Carver was a boy. Maybe this tree saw his secret garden!"

I did, I did! I say, but they don't hear me as they move down the path to see the Carver house on the farm where George grew up. Maybe someday you'll come and visit me at the George Washington Carver National Monument in Diamond, Missouri.

I don't know what a computer is, but the ranger says that you can use one to learn more about the park. Since George Washington Carver always loved to learn, I wonder if he would have loved computers as much as he loved books. What do you think?

FOR FURTHER DISCUSSION

Dear Parents, Teachers, and Children,
    In order to write this book, I visited the George Washington Carver National Monument twice, read books about George Washington Carver, and consulted with staff at the park. When I read a final draft to children in grades K–3, I noticed that kindergartners and first graders did not ask historical questions, but some second and third graders did. Complicated answers can be saved for children at an older age. All of the children in grades K–3 loved responding to my two questions to them: What kind of great American would you like to be someday? How could you become that person?   *Jean Marzollo*

Do trees live longer than people?
Trees can live much longer. Trees can live for hundreds of years.

Can trees really tell stories?
No, but it's fun to use your imagination and pretend that they can tell what they "saw" long ago. If you learn something about the history of people where you live, maybe you too can write a "tree" story.

Why are Uncle Moses and Aunt Sue white?
For children age 6 and younger: People who study people who lived long ago are called historians. Historians don't know exactly what happened to George's parents. They think that his father died; they don't know what happened to his mother. George was taken care of by Moses and Sue Carver, who owned the farm where George lived. George and his brother called them Uncle and Aunt. *For children age 7 and older:* Moses Carver had a small farm in southwest Missouri at the time of the Civil War. This was a place and a time where some, but not all, white farmers enslaved African Americans. These farmers bought slaves, gave them food and shelter, but did not pay them for their work. George's mother was owned by Uncle Moses. George and his mother were kidnapped when George was a baby, maybe by people who wanted slaves but didn't want to pay for them. Moses Carver sent someone to find George and his mother, but only George was found. George's father, who was enslaved by a nearby farmer, died when George was a baby. Slavery was finally outlawed in the United States in 1865. George was about one year old then. So he was born a slave, but he did not grow up as a slave.

Why couldn't Little George go to school?
Where he lived, there was no school for black children. Laws and customs kept many black and white children in separate schools. Since then these laws and customs have changed.

Did George Washington Carver know Martin Luther King?

Martin Luther King, Jr., was fourteen years old when George Washington Carver died in 1943. He probably knew about George Washington Carver because by then Dr. Carver was known all over the country, especially in the black community. Martin Luther King, Jr., grew up to be a pastor who helped the United States change bad laws such as those that said that black and white children could not go to the same schools.

Martin Luther King, Jr., was born on January 15, 1929. We celebrate his birthday on Martin Luther King, Jr. Day. We don't know the exact year when George Carver was born because birth records were not always kept for slaves. (That's why there's a *c.* before his birth year date. The *c.* means "around." He was born around the year 1864.) We do know that he died on January 5, 1943, so we call January 5 George Washington Carver Recognition Day.

Where did George Washington Carver go to college?

He went to Simpson College in Iowa and to Iowa Agricultural College (now Iowa State University), where he was the first black student.

"My work, my life, must be in the spirit of a little child seeking only to know the truth and follow it."
—George Washington Carver
(c. 1864-1943)

Tuskegee University Archives

Did George Washington Carver really invent three hundred uses for peanuts? Did he invent peanut butter?

He found more than three hundred uses for peanuts, such as peanut milk and peanut oil, but he did not invent peanut butter. Dr. Carver liked teaching people about different uses for peanuts because he wanted farmers to try growing them, as well as cotton.

Did Dr. Carver like teaching?

He loved learning, and he loved teaching. He taught plant science (botany) and agriculture.

How can we use a computer to find out more about the park where Little George lived?

Just go to www.nps.gov/gwca. You'll find pictures and information about the park and George Washington Carver. Maybe you'll get to visit the park someday.

Peanut Plant

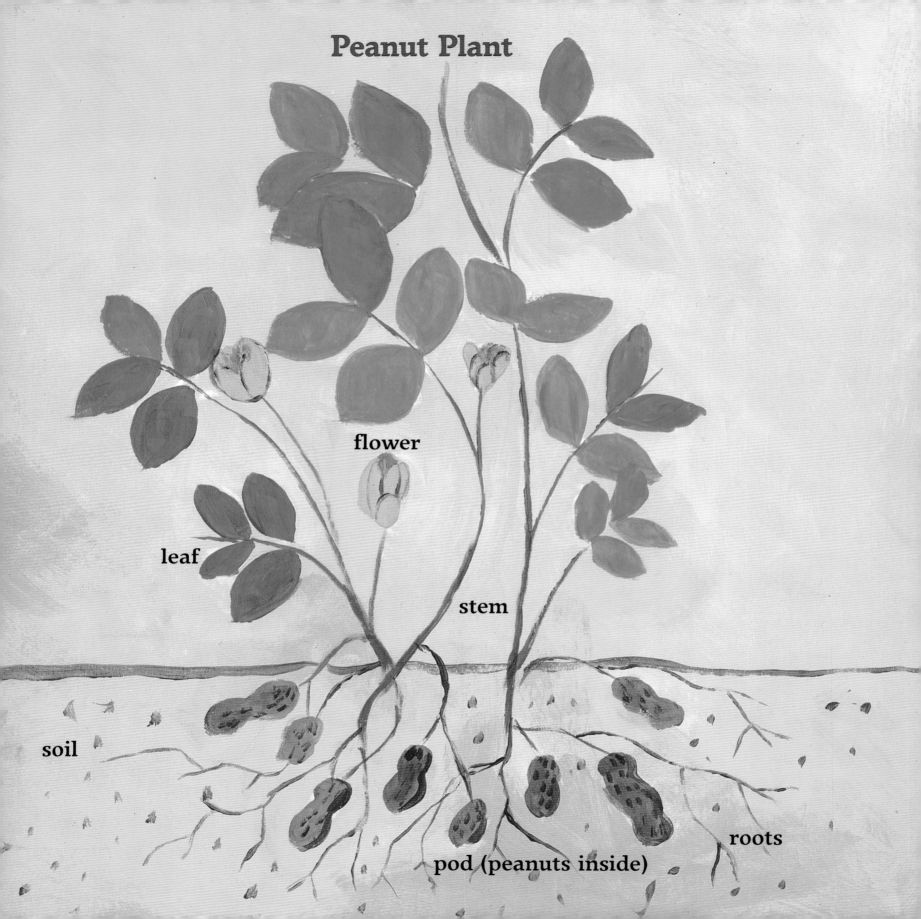

flower

leaf

stem

soil

pod (peanuts inside)

roots